EASY GUITAR WITH NOTES & TAB

BRUNO MARS
UNORTHODOX JUKEBOX

ISBN 978-1-4803-5365-7

HAL•LEONARD® CORPORATION

7777 W. BLUEMOUND RD. P.O. BOX 13819 MILWAUKEE, WI 53213

In Australia Contact:
Hal Leonard Australia Pty. Ltd.
4 Lentara Court
Cheltenham, Victoria, 3192 Australia
Email: ausadmin@halleonard.com.au

Visit Hal Leonard Online at
www.halleonard.com

Young Girls

Words and Music by Bruno Mars, Ari Levine, Philip Lawrence, Jeff Bhasker and Emile Haynie

*Capo IV

Strum Pattern: 5
Pick Pattern: 1

Intro
Moderately

*Optional: To match recording, place capo at 4th fret.

Verse

all my mon-ey on a big old fan-cy car
2. *See additional lyrics*

for these bright-eyed hon-eys. Oh yeah,

1. I spend

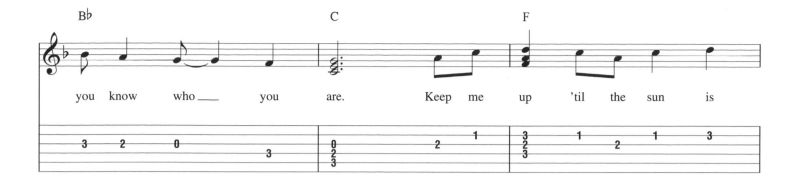

you know who __ you are. Keep me up 'til the sun is

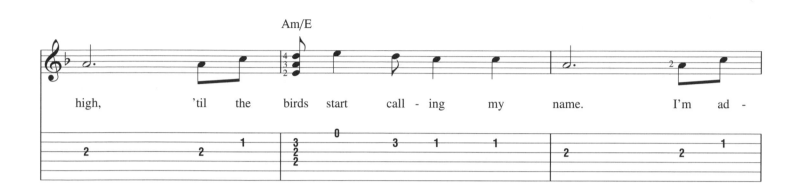

high, 'til the birds start call - ing my name. I'm ad -

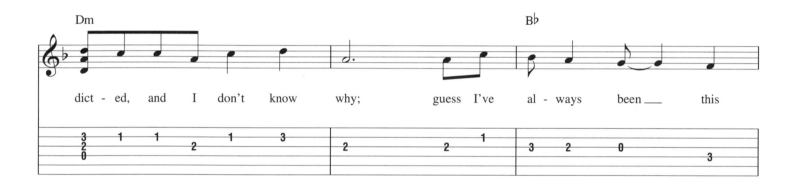

dict - ed, and I don't know why; guess I've al - ways been __ this

Pre-Chorus

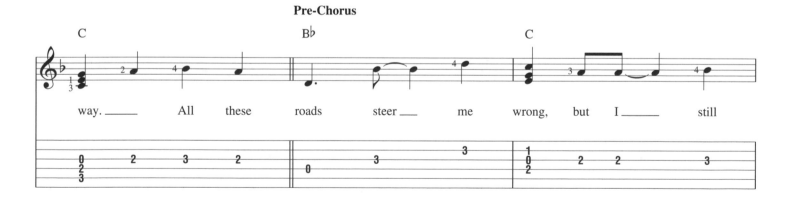

way. ____ All these roads steer __ me wrong, but I ____ still

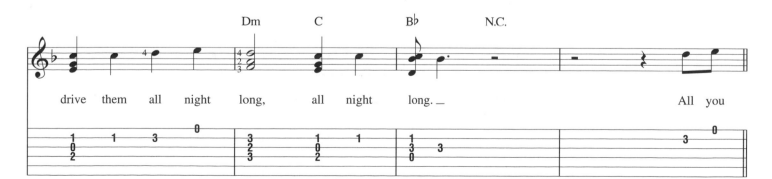

drive them all night long, all night long. __ All you

3

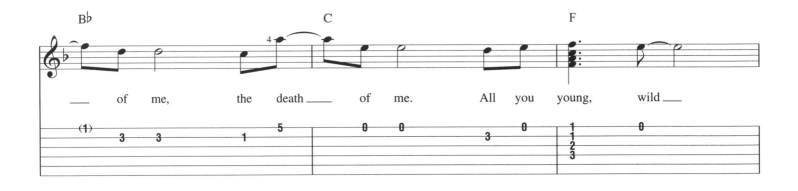

4

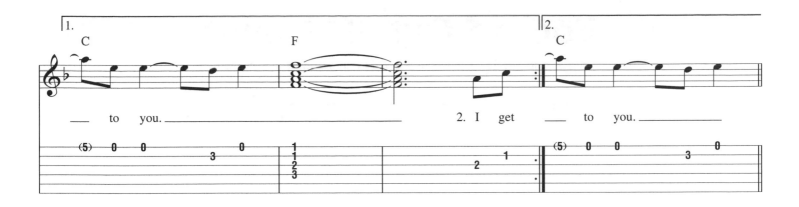

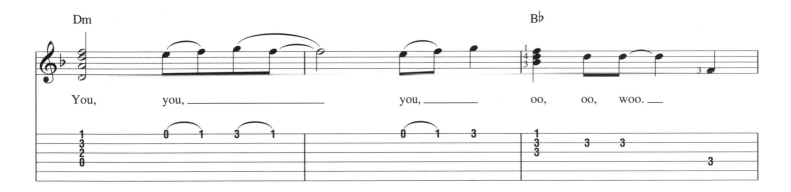

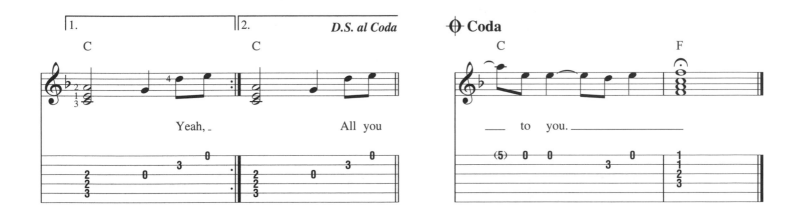

Additional Lyrics

2. I get lost under these lights;
I get lost in the words I say,
Start believing my own lies
Like ev'rything will be okay.
Oh, I still dream of a simple life:
Boy meets girl, makes her his wife.
But love don't exist when you live like this;
That much I know, yes, I know.

Locked Out of Heaven

Words and Music by Bruno Mars, Ari Levine and Philip Lawrence

*Capo III

Strum Pattern: 5
Pick Pattern: 5

Intro
Moderately fast

*Optional: To match recording, place capo at 3rd fret.

*Lyrics in italic are spoken throughout.

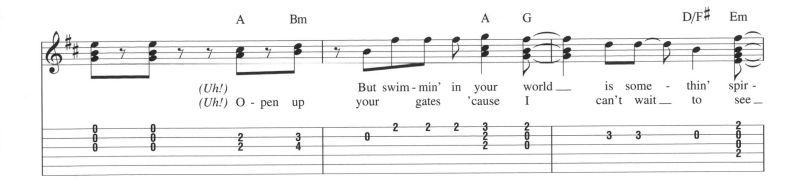

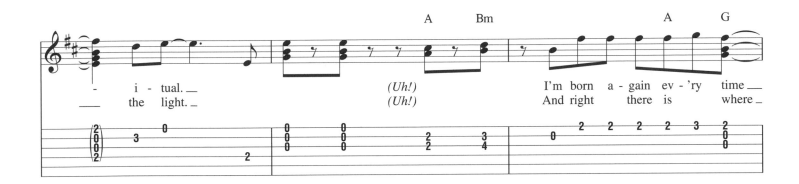

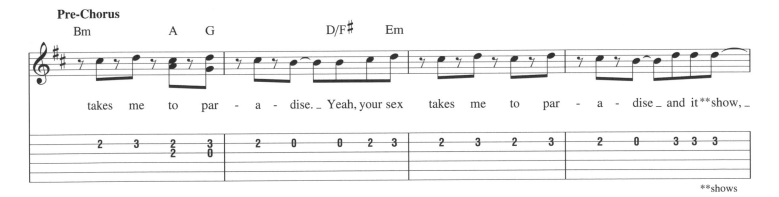

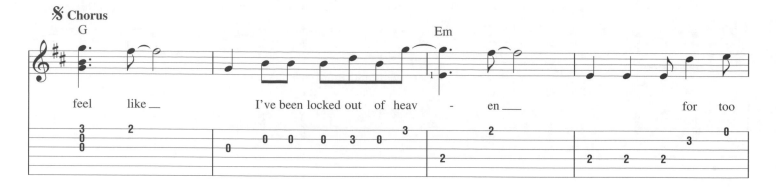

feel like __ I've been locked out of heav - en __ for too

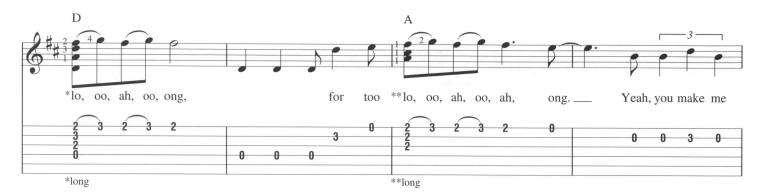

*lo, oo, ah, oo, ong, for too **lo, oo, ah, oo, ah, ong. __ Yeah, you make me

*long **long

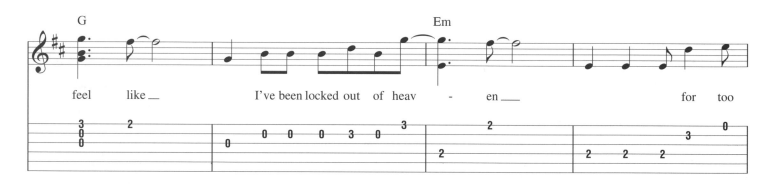

feel like __ I've been locked out of heav - en __ for too

1.

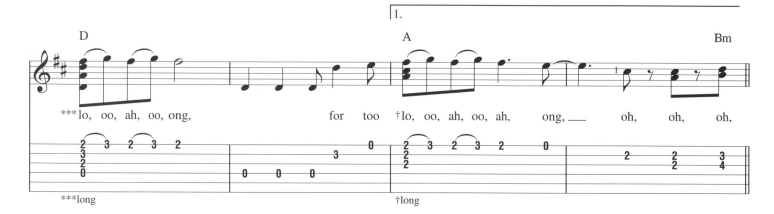

***lo, oo, ah, oo, ong, for too †lo, oo, ah, oo, ah, ong, __ oh, oh, oh,

***long †long

Interlude

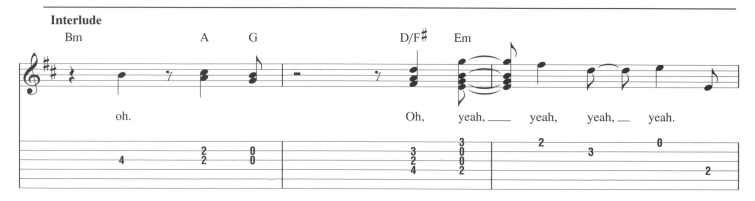

oh. Oh, yeah, __ yeah, yeah, __ yeah.

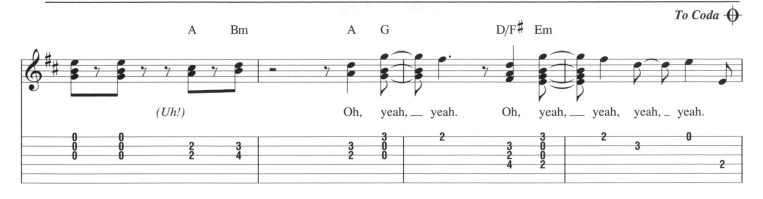

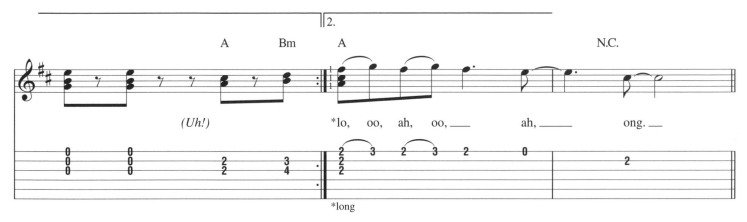

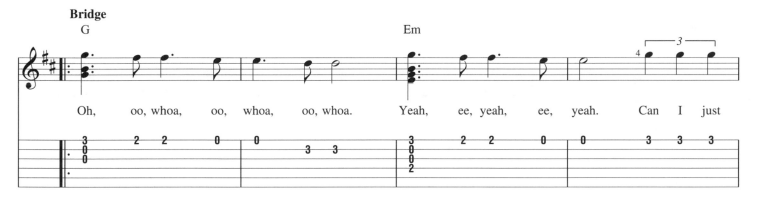

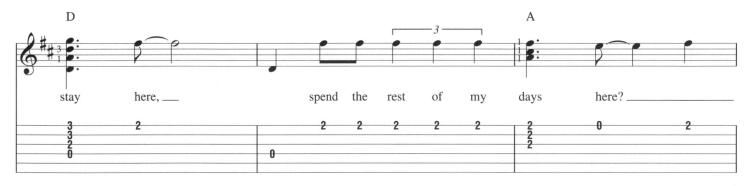

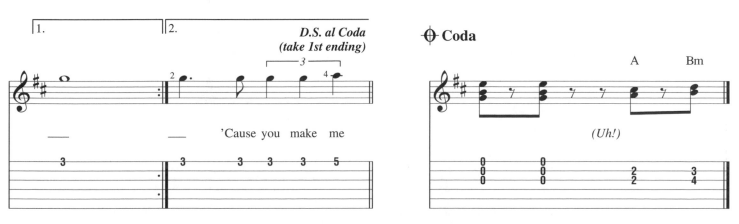

Gorilla

Words and Music by Bruno Mars, Ari Levine and Philip Lawrence

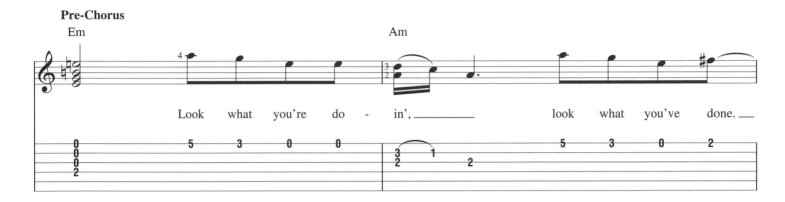

Chorus

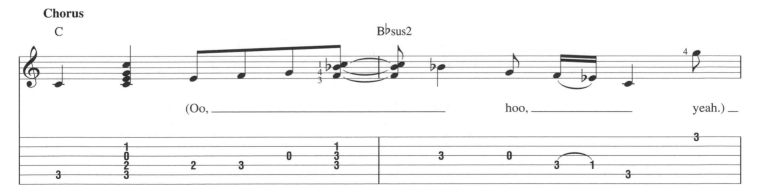

You and me, ba - by, mak - in' love like go - ril - las.

(Oo, _____ hoo, _____ yeah.) ___

You and me, ba - by, mak - in' love like go - ril - las.

Bridge

I bet you nev - er ev - er felt ___ so good, ___ so good. ___

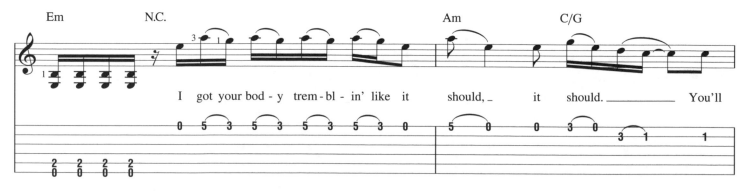

I got your bod - y trem - bl - in' like it should, ___ it should. _____ You'll

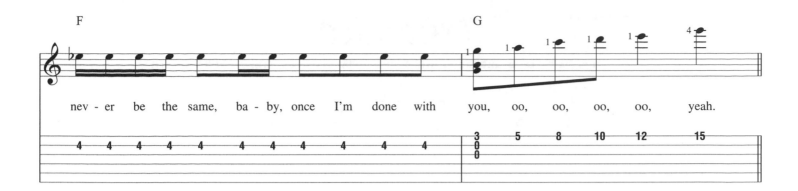

nev-er be the same, ba-by, once I'm done with you, oo, oo, oo, oo, yeah.

Chorus
1st time, w/ Voc. ad lib.

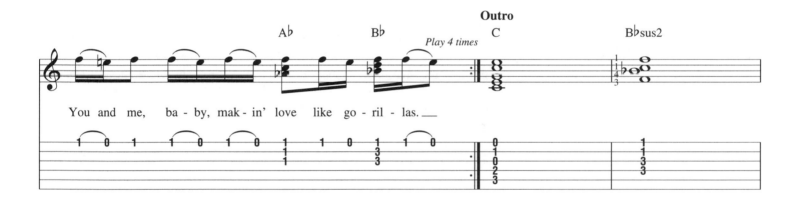

(Oo, _____ hoo, _____ yeah.) _____

Outro

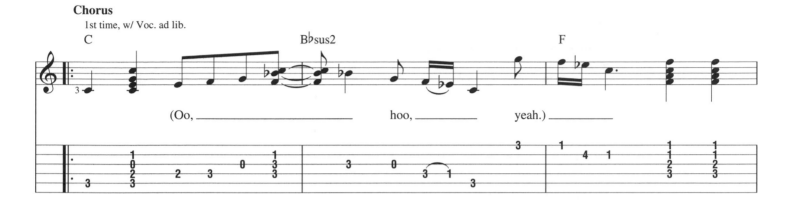

You and me, ba-by, mak-in' love like go-ril-las. __

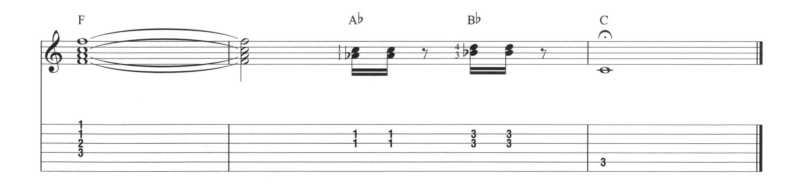

Additional Lyrics

2. Yeah, got a fistful of your hair,
But you don't look like you're scared;
You just smile and tell me, "Daddy, it's yours,"
'Cause you know how I like it. You's a dirty little lover.
If the neighbors call the cops, call the sheriff, call the S.W.A.T.,
We don't stop. We keep rockin' while they're knockin' on our door.
And you're screamin',
"Give it to me baby, give it to me motherfucker."

Treasure

Words and Music by Bruno Mars, Ari Levine, Philip Lawrence and Phredley Brown

*Capo III

Strum Pattern: 5
Pick Pattern: 1

*Optional: To match recording, place capo at 3rd fret.   **Strum muted strings.

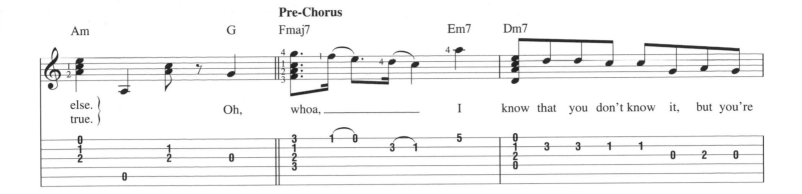

Pre-Chorus

else.
true.

Oh, whoa, _____ I know that you don't know it, but you're

fine, so fine. _ (Fine, so fine.) _ Oh, whoa, _____ oh,

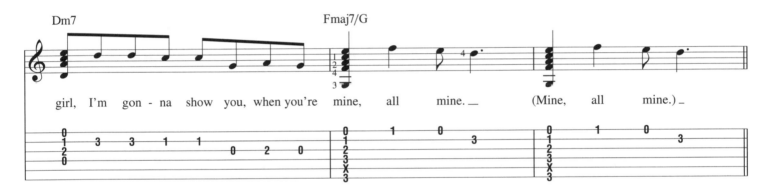

girl, I'm gon - na show you, when you're mine, all mine. _ (Mine, all mine.) _

Chorus

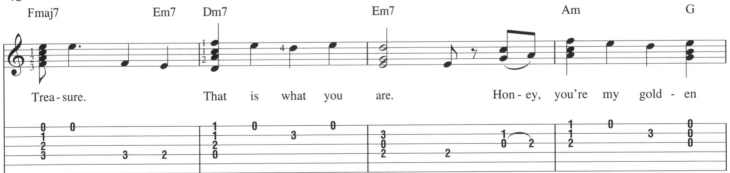

Trea - sure. That is what you are. Hon - ey, you're my gold - en

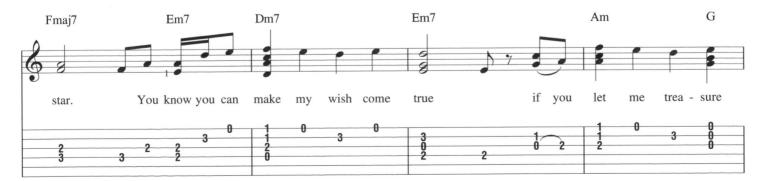

star. You know you can make my wish come true if you let me trea - sure

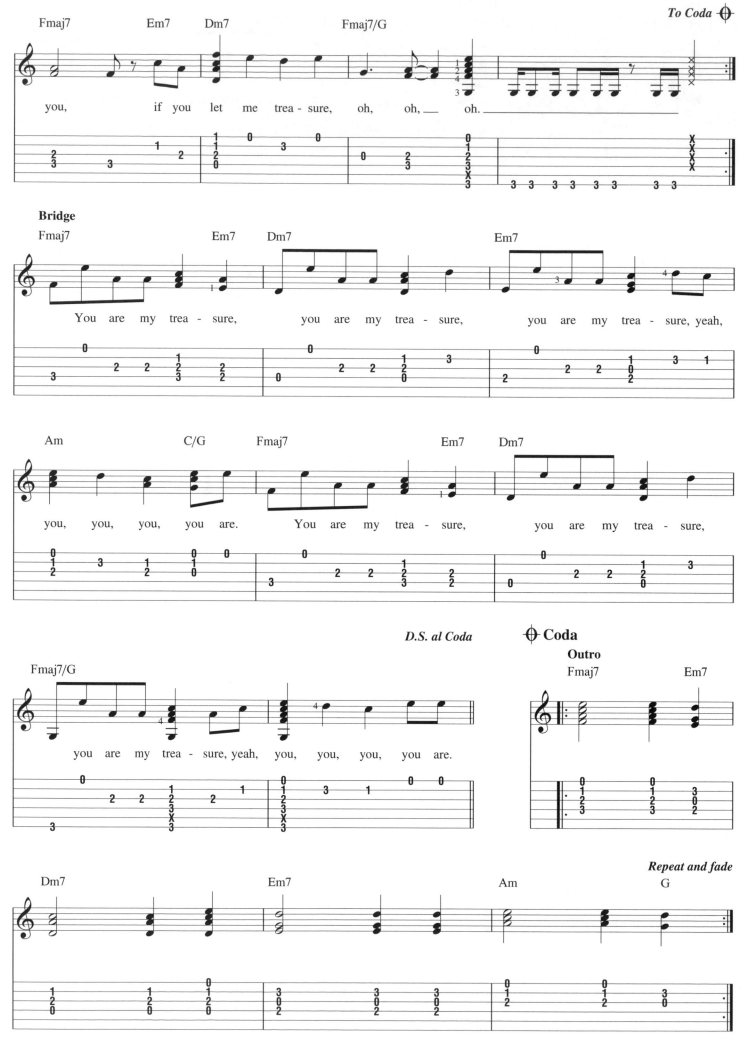

Natalie

Words and Music by Bruno Mars, Ari Levine, Philip Lawrence, Paul Epworth and Benjamin Levin

*Optional: To match recording, place capo at 5th fret.

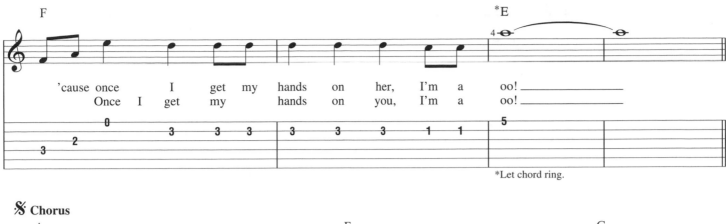

'cause once I get my hands on her, I'm a oo! _____
Once I get my hands on you, I'm a oo! _____

*Let chord ring.

𝄋 Chorus

Nat - a - lie. ___ She ran a - way with all my mon - ey, _____

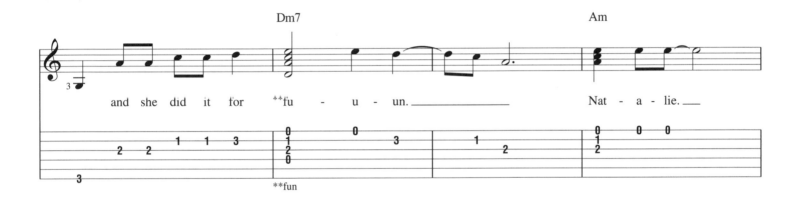

and she did it for **fu - u - un. _____ Nat - a - lie. ___

**fun

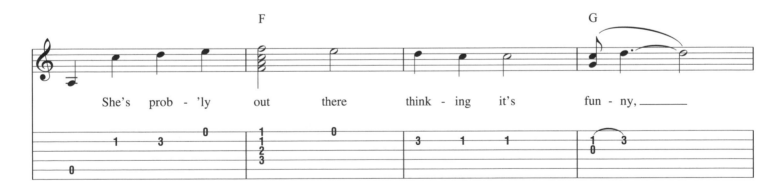

She's prob - 'ly out there think - ing it's fun - ny, _____

tell - in' ***ev - 'ry - o - o - one. _____ Well, I'm dig -

***ev'ryone

gin' my ditch for this gold ___ dig-gin' bitch. Watch out, ___ she's quick.

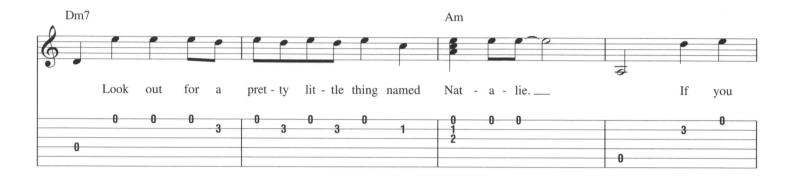

Look out for a pret-ty lit-tle thing named Nat - a - lie. ___ If you

To Coda

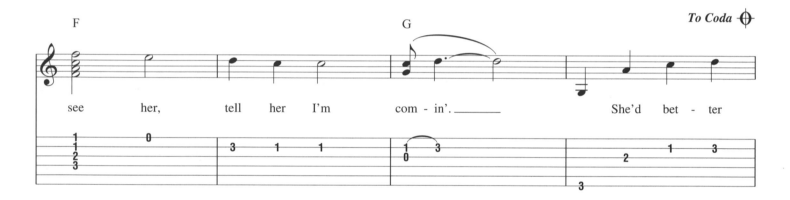

see her, tell her I'm com-in'. ___ She'd bet - ter

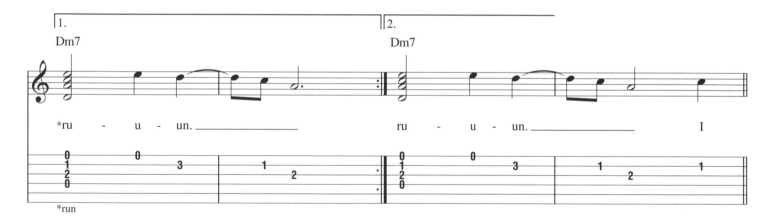

1.
*ru - u - un. ___ ru - u - un. ___ I

*run

Bridge

should -'ve known ___ bet - ter (I should -'ve known ___ bet - ter) 'cause

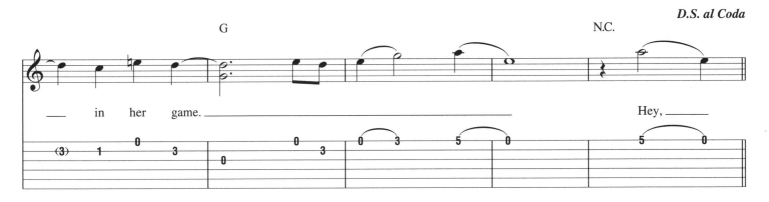

Moonshine

Words and Music by Bruno Mars, Ari Levine, Philip Lawrence, Jeff Bhasker, Andrew Wyatt and Mark Ronson

*Optional: To match recording, place capo at 5th fret.

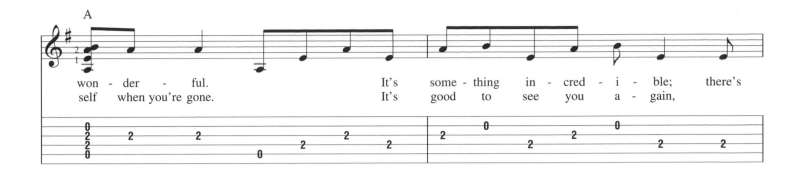

won - der - ful.   It's some - thing in - cred - i - ble; there's
self when you're gone.   It's good to see you a - gain,

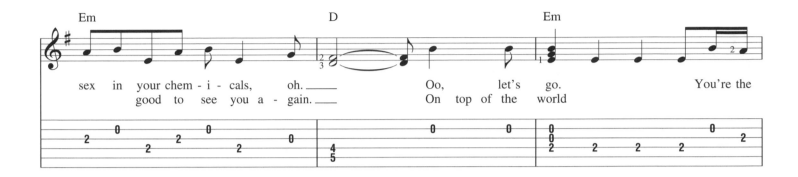

sex in your chem - i - cals, oh. _____   Oo, let's go.   You're the
good to see you a - gain. _____   On top of the world

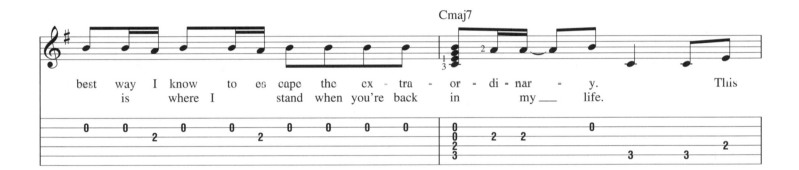

best way I know to es - cape the ex - tra - or - di - nar - y.   This
is where I stand when you're back in my _____ life.

world ain't for you, and I know for damn sure this world ain't for me.
Life's not so bad _____ when you're way up this high; _____

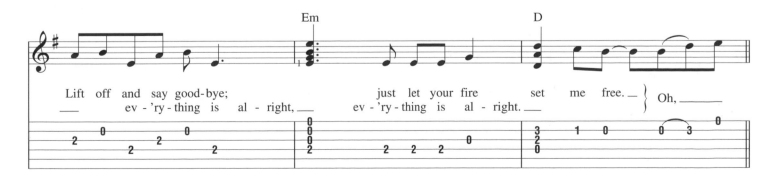

Lift off and say good-bye;   just let your fire set me free. _____
_____ ev - 'ry-thing is al - right, _____   ev - 'ry-thing is al - right. _____   Oh, _____

Bridge

Don't look down, don't you nev-er look back. Me, I'm not a-fraid to die

young and live fast. Give me good times, give me love, give me laughs. Let's

D.S. al Coda
(take 2nd ending)

take a ride through the sky be-fore the night is gone.

Let chord ring.

Coda

Outro

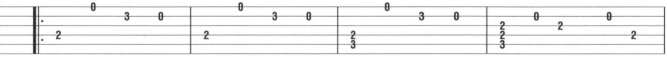

Repeat and fade

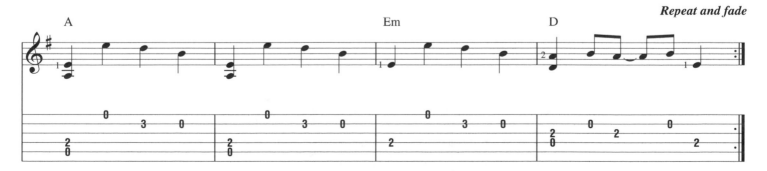

25

When I Was Your Man

Words and Music by Bruno Mars, Ari Levine, Philip Lawrence and Andrew Wyatt

*Optional: To match recording, place capo at 5th fret.

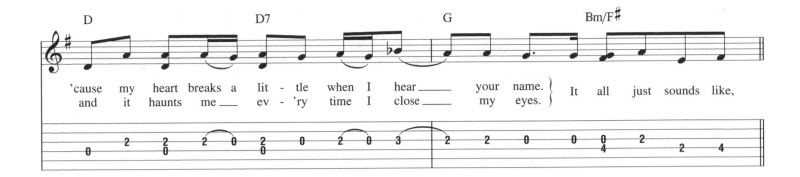

'cause my heart breaks a lit-tle when I hear your name. It all just sounds like,
and it haunts me ev-'ry time I close my eyes.

Pre-Chorus

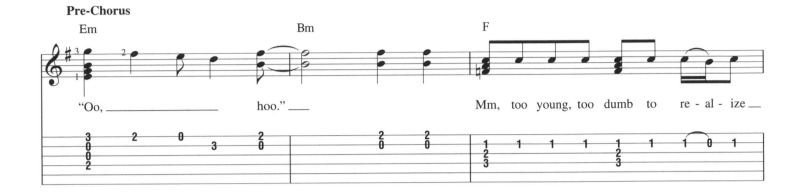

"Oo, hoo." Mm, too young, too dumb to re-al-ize

Chorus

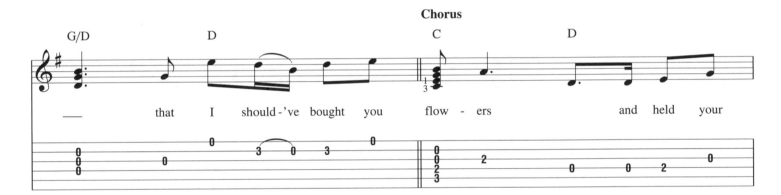

that I should-'ve bought you flow-ers and held your

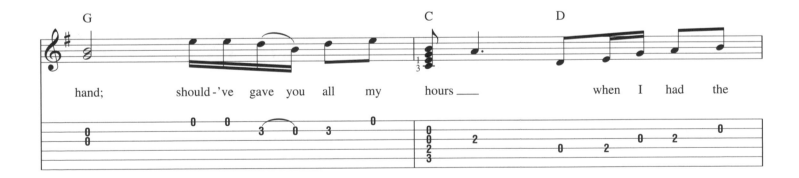

hand; should-'ve gave you all my hours when I had the

chance; take you to ev-'ry par-ty, 'cause all you want-ed to do was

dance. _____ Now my ba - by's danc - ing, _____ but she's danc - ing with an - oth - er

man. man. Al - though it

Bridge

hurts, I'll be the first _____ to say that _____ I was wrong. _____

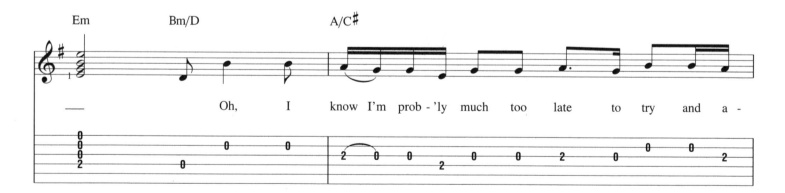

_____ Oh, I know I'm prob - 'ly much too late to try and a -

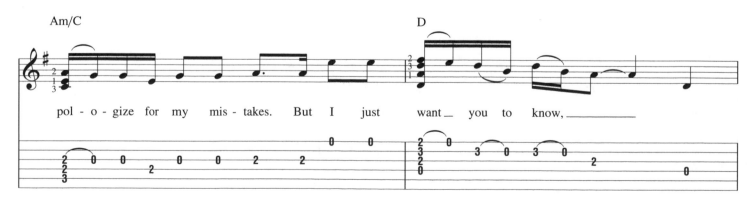

pol - o - gize for my mis - takes. But I just want _____ you to know, _____

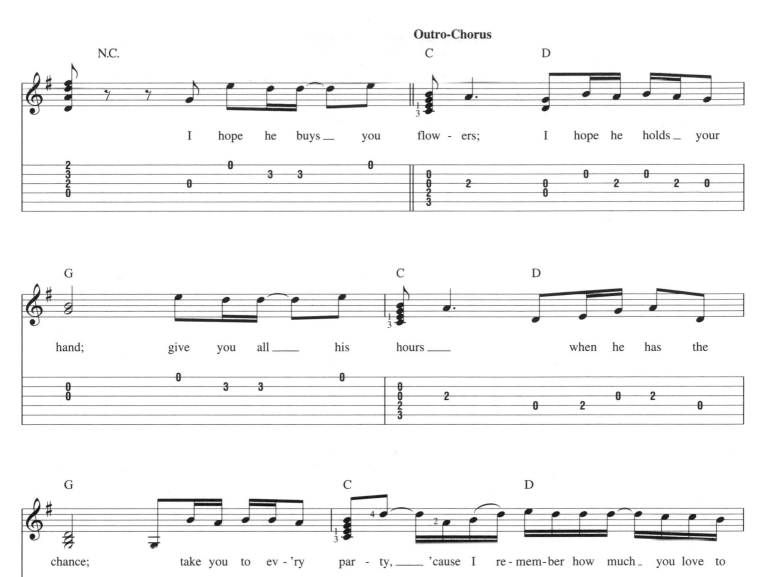

I hope he buys _ you flow - ers; I hope he holds _ your

hand; give you all _ his hours _ when he has the

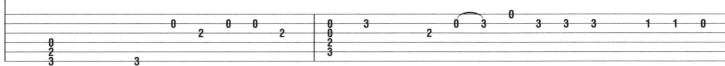

chance; take you to ev - 'ry par - ty, _ 'cause I re - mem - ber how much _ you love to

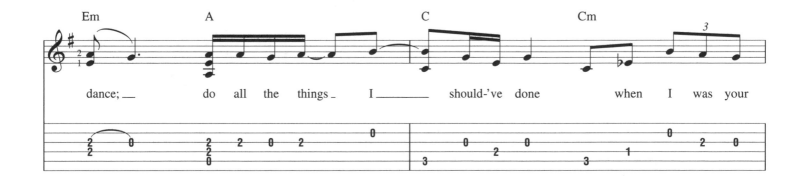

dance; _ do all the things _ I _ should-'ve done when I was your

man. Do all the things _ I _ should-'ve done when I was your man.

Show Me

Words and Music by Bruno Mars, Ari Levine, Philip Lawrence, Dwayne "Supa Dups" Chin-Quee and Mitchum Chin

Strum Pattern: 1
Pick Pattern: 2

Intro
Moderately slow, in 2

*Bass arr. for gtr.

Verse

1. I can see it in your eyes, you want a good time, you wan-na put your
2. Love, the way that you laugh, the way that you smile, makes me feel

bod - y on mine. Al - right, but don't change your mind, don't you change it,
like you've been wait - ing a while. Well guess what dar - ling, I've been wait -

oh, no. _____ Oh, yeah, you called me to -
ing too. _____ So let's ride; _____

day,   drove all this   way,   so don't let this   buzz   go   to   waste,   oh,
we can get freak - y   to - night; _____ right here's your tick - et   to

no.   Your plea - sure, plea - sure   is - land   is   where   we   can _____ go. _____
ride. _____ Tell   me   girl, what   you   gon' _____ do? _____

Pre-Chorus

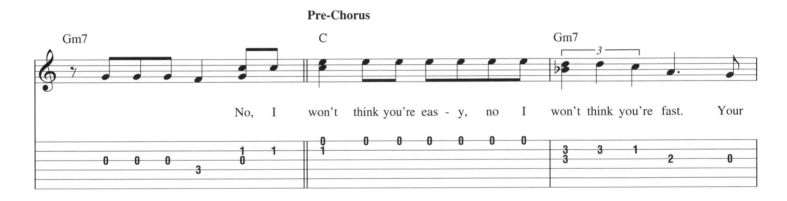

No,   I   won't think you're eas - y,   no   I   won't think you're fast.   Your

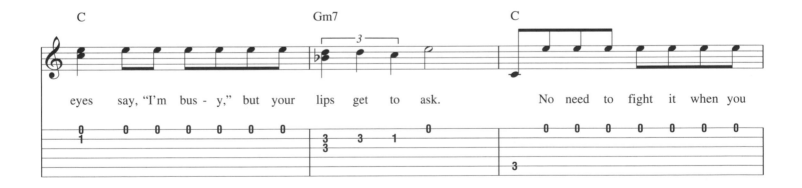

eyes   say, "I'm bus - y," but your   lips   get   to   ask.   No need to fight it when you

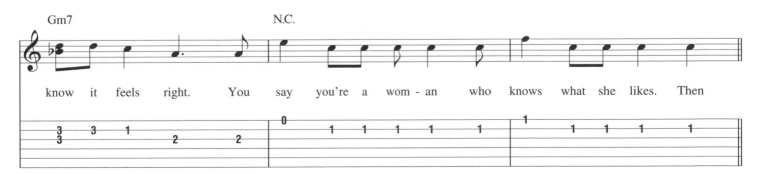

know   it feels right.   You   say you're a wom - an   who   knows   what   she   likes.   Then

% Chorus

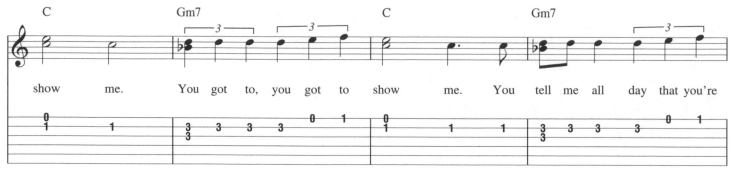

show me.　　You got to, you got to show　　me.　　You tell me all　day　that you're

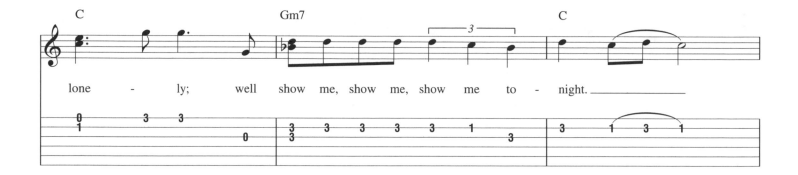

lone - ly;　well show me, show me, show me to - night. _____

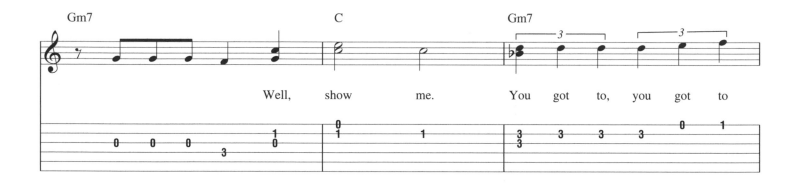

Well,　show　me.　　You　got　to,　you　got　to

show　　me.　　You　tell　me　all　day　that　you're　lone　-　ly;　well

To Coda ⊕ | 1.

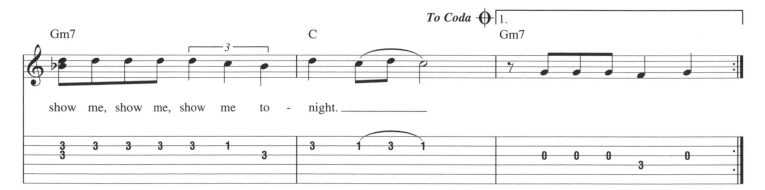

show me, show me, show　me　to - night. _____

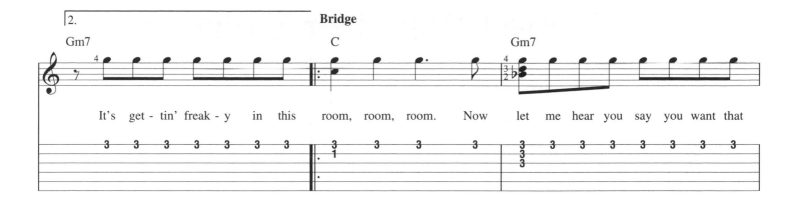

It's gettin' freak-y in this room, room, room. Now let me hear you say you want that

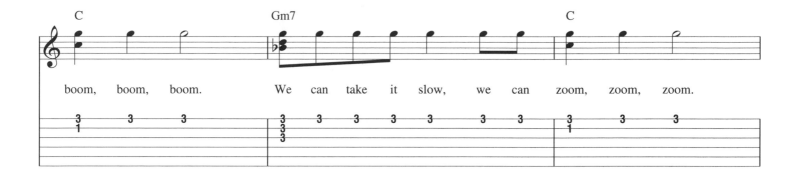

boom, boom, boom. We can take it slow, we can zoom, zoom, zoom.

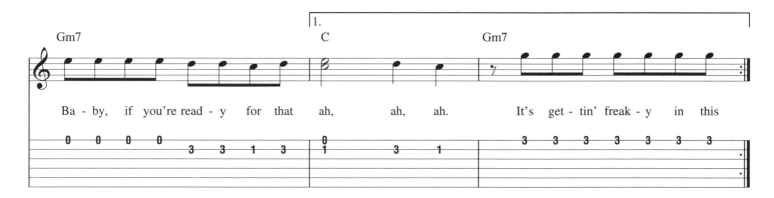

Ba-by, if you're read-y for that ah, ah, ah. It's gettin' freak-y in this

D.S. al Coda **Coda**

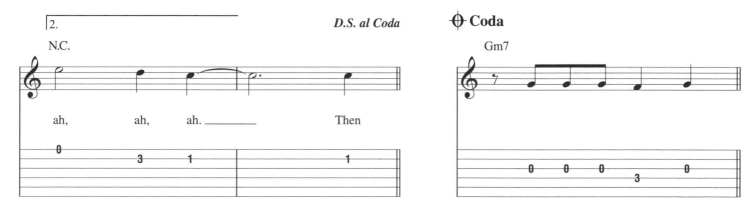

ah, ah, ah._____ Then

Outro

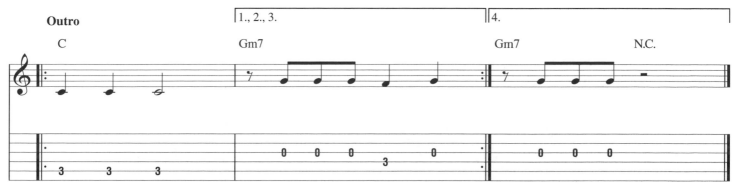

Money Make Her Smile

Words and Music by Bruno Mars, Ari Levine, Philip Lawrence and Christopher Brown

let   you   down.   Watch her drop it   like...   hey.
dol - lars   fall.

Interlude

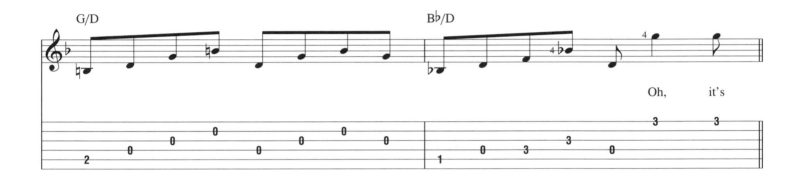

Oh,   it's

 Pre-Chorus

not com - pli - cat - ed, so this won't take a while. You see,

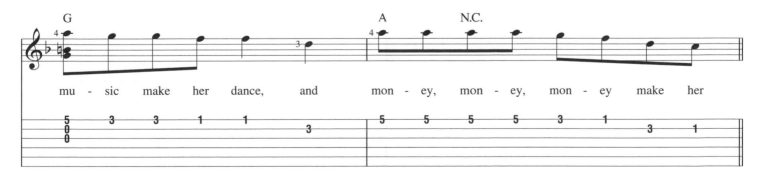

mu - sic make her dance,   and   mon - ey, mon - ey, mon - ey make her

Yeah. Yeah. Watch her.

Bridge

Dm
*

*Bass arr. for gtr.

(Give her what you got, give her, give her what you got, got, got, got, got.

D.S. al Coda

Give her what you got, give her, give her what you got, got, got.) Oh, it's

⊕ Coda

B♭/D   N.C.

Mon-ey, mon-ey, mon-ey make her smile.

If I Knew

Words and Music by Bruno Mars, Ari Levine and Philip Lawrence

*Optional: To match recording, place capo at 3rd fret.

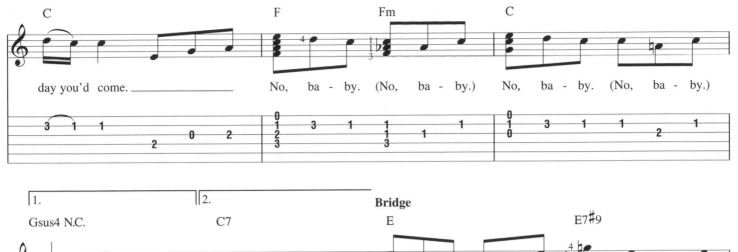

day you'd come. ____ No, ba-by. (No, ba-by.) No, ba-by. (No, ba-by.)

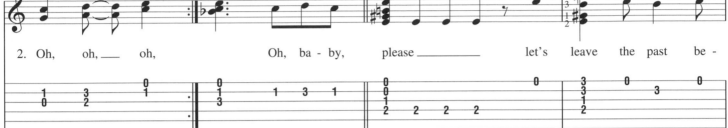

1. **2.** **Bridge**

2. Oh, oh, ___ oh, Oh, ba-by, please ____ let's leave the past be-

hind us, ____ be-hind us, ____ so that we ____ can

go where love will find us, ____ yeah, will find us. ____ I know

most ___ girls would leave me, ___ but I know that you'll be-lieve me. 3. Ba-by,

I, _____ I wish we were sev - en - teen _____

so I could give you all the in - no - cence ___

that you give to me. ___ Oh, I would-n't have done _____ all ___

___ the things ___ that I've done ___ if I knew _____ one

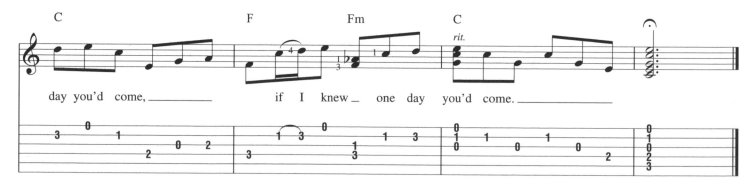

day you'd come, _____ if I knew ___ one day you'd come. _____